C.K. SPADES

WORK FOR YOURSELF

The Ultimate Guide to Creating Your Own Job and Working For Yourself, Learn the Ways on How You Can Create Your Own Job So You Don't Need to Look For One Anymore

Descrierea CIP a Bibliotecii Naționale a României
C.K. SPADES
   WORK FOR YOURSELF. The Ultimate Guide to Creating Your Own Job and Working For Yourself, Learn the Ways on How You Can Create Your Own Job So You Don't Need to Look For One Anymore / C.K. Spades – Bucharest: Editura My Ebook, 2021
ISBN

C.K. SPADES

WORK FOR YOURSELF

The Ultimate Guide to Creating Your Own Job and Working For Yourself, Learn the Ways on How You Can Create Your Own Job So You Don't Need to Look For One Anymore

My Ebook Publishing House
Bucharest, 2021

CONTENTS

The Truth about the Job Market …………………..	7
Why do freelance? Realistic expectations …………….	14
How do I get started? ……………………………………...	19
Online Freelance & Subcontracting …………………….	35
Freelancing Websites ……………………………………...	49
How To Market Yourself ………………………………….	78
Advanced Technique: Making The Sale ………………..	90
Payment options what's next? ………………………….	101
Last But Not Least ………………………………………..	119

THE TRUTH ABOUT THE JOB MARKET

It's no secret that the job market is more volatile and unpredictable than ever these days. Depending on where you live, the unemployment rates can fluctuate from a reasonable 7% to as high as 25% and who knows exactly how high they could go in the near future.

Finding a job is almost impossible. Companies everywhere are cutting costs and downsizing like there's no tomorrow. For many companies there really is no tomorrow; even the "Fail-proof" companies are seeing bankruptcies and buyouts more often than ever in the past 100 years! If you don't already have a steady, stable job with a well-established company then you definitely picked the wrong decade to be unemployed in. Even if you have a stable job there's really no telling if it will be there next month, or even next week.

So what's the solution? What can do you? You can't just magically change the economy and make the job market better; you probably won't get a lot done by writing a letter to your senator either. Believe it or not there is a solution and it requires a lot of work and dedication but it's a lot better than being unemployed.

Create your own job! I know, that sounds a little funny when you just look at it like that but it's the truth. There are no jobs out there and the few that are open are only going to highly qualified people with years of experience so unless you fit that category you have to create your own job. Specifically I'm talking about freelancing.

People have been doing freelancing for thousands of years; even in ancient Rome the army hired mercenaries to go into battle when there weren't enough soldiers. Mercenaries were freelance warriors; they weren't employed full-time by a

particular nation's army - they just worked for whoever was willing to pay the most.

Hopefully you don't have to do any paid fighting any time soon but the spirit of the mercenary and the idea of contract work carries on thousands of years later in the form of freelancing. By becoming your own boss and establishing contract relationships you open up a world of money-making possibilities while completely abandoning all of the negative aspects that come with a typical, "9 to 5" job.

In this book we're going to explore the many options you have should you choose to become a freelancer. We're going to talk about freelance work in a way that allows you to learn the essential techniques regardless of what field you choose to freelance in, be it business, graphic design or even housekeeping!

So what's so great about freelance work exactly? Well, let me start out by giving you an example of the type of person freelancing is NOT good for. If the following paragraph describes your life then you can stop reading this and just go back to what you were doing.

Do you enjoy getting up early, every single morning and wading through miles of traffic to get to work? Do you find it exciting seeing the exact same people every single day, five to six days a week with absolutely no variety or change? Are you your boss' best friend? Do you look forward to answering to your boss and having to meet his or her deadlines constantly? Do you enjoy never seeing your family members during the day or always having to miss out on events like school recitals and soccer games? Is it fun to make poverty-level wages and live paycheck to paycheck so that you pretty much have no variety in your life because any big expense could make your bills come crashing down on you?

If you answered yes to all of those questions then, as I said, stop reading and go back to your "wonderful" life - freelance work probably isn't for you. If you did freelance work you'd be your own boss; you'd be taking your career into your own hands and having complete control over your life. You can just throw this book away or delete it from your hard drive.

Now, if you didn't' answer yes to all of those questions you might be the type of person who could have a lucrative career freelancing. Get comfortable, grab a pen and a pad of paper so you can take some notes and get ready to explore one of the most rewarding and lucrative ways of making a living in the 21st century.

Does freelancing mean you will get rich overnight? No, it takes work and dedication. There are a number of obstacles that you will have to overcome but the rewards will be substantial if you are willing to put in the time and effort. The possibilities are endless. There are opportunities for any person to break into the lucrative career of freelancing. All you need is diligence, patience, and tenacity to pursue it and make it happen. This book will show you how.

On the other hand, if you are the person that was described at the beginning of the chapter, get that beverage and curl up with the latest novel by your favorite author. It might be enjoyable reading and that is fine. Just remember, unless you are doing that for a living, you won't be making a dime.

Be Your Own Boss

Freelancing allows you to be your own boss. This means you make your own hours. Making your own hours does not mean loafing around all day. It means having the self-discipline to set aside a certain amount of hours that you work each day. But, as the boss, you get to decide what those hours are. That way you can pick up the kids from school, have lunch with the spouse, go to the gym during the day when it's not so crowded, and never have to make that horrible rush-hour commute.

Wear what you want. Does your current job have a dress code? How does sitting in your pajamas all day sound; what about just spending the day wearing your favorite pair of worn out jeans and that T-shirt from that unforgettable 1980's rock concert. If you are an independent agent, like a freelancer, then you decide the dress code.

Set Your Own Price

Being a freelancer means that you get to set your own prices for what your time is worth. You get to determine your own prices based on your costs and your time. You don't have to pay yourself a minimum amount or charge a certain amount; you have total control over what kind of money you can make. Instead of waiting years to get a raise you can adjust your own prices. As you become more proficient and widen your client base you can double and triple your earnings as you see fit.

Live Wherever You Want

Have you ever considered living somewhere else but your job and family obligations keep you stuck in the same place.

Freelancing gives you the freedom to take your family, if that applies to you or just yourself and live wherever you want. As long as you have a phone, a computer and a way to receive mail, you can live at the South Pole or Hawaii and still have a lucrative freelancing career. Your home is your office. You can be sitting in a coffee shop and enjoying a scone with a mocha latte at the same time you are making millions of dollars.

REALISTIC EXPECTATIONS

A lot of people live by two very popular, old saying: "Nothing in life is free," and "If it sounds too good to be true then it probably is." In the case of freelancing, the price is minimal. As you will see in future chapters you will need some general items such as a computer, a printer and maybe a fax and scanner. After you have the materials needed to be a freelancer your greatest cost will be your time and effort. How much are you worth? The best part is that you get to decide what your time and effort are worth.

As far as the rule "if it sounds too good to be true it probably is," here is something to consider. You should not quit your day job immediately and hope to make $10,000 next month. Instead, start slow and work your way to making the money you want. If you are making the equivalent of your full time job and you have too much freelance work to do, then decide to freelance full time and quit your day job. If you work hard this process can happen rather quickly, so don't be discouraged. The jobs are real. The money is real. The only investment is the amount of time you are willing to invest.

The market for freelancers is growing in leaps and bounds. The future markets are projected to continue to grow at the same rapid rate. This means more fantastic freelance opportunities and greater potential income. Companies love working with freelancers because they're a lot more convenient and often a lot less expensive than hiring traditional employees. When a company hires a freelancer the freelancer worries about the materials and methods in completing the project. The company (or individual) only has to be concerned with communicating their needs to the contractor (another word for freelancer) and approving the final results. Freelancers don't have to be hired out from temp agencies, given benefits for meeting work hour requirements or any other formalities that employees require. Because of this and thanks to the trend of downsizing and cutting employees, freelancing is becoming more active and profitable than ever!

Let's do a brief overview of the pros and cons to give you a clear image of what you can expect when getting into freelancing.

The Pros

- Be your own boss, set your own hours
- Never get fired - you only have to look for new clients
- Work when you want and how you want, no limits
- Work thousands of miles away, no distance barriers.
- Spend more time with your family and friends
- Potentially make a lot more money than a "9 to 5" job.
- Economy affects job availability differently; usually a poor economy increases freelance work rather than decrease it.

The Cons

- No work is guaranteed - you're always looking for clients.
- Profits will be slow until you build up your business.
- In the U.S. you will have to pay more taxes.
- You must be skilled or a professional; there's no freelance hamburger flipping.

While there are definitely some caveats to be had about freelancing you can see that there are more pros than cons and honestly the pros outweigh the cons, for most people anyway. The versatility of freelance jobs makes them a powerful choice for anyone who's had trouble holding down a steady job with their local economy.

Who Freelance Works For

If you're the type of person who likes to have a different thing to do every day and loves variety then freelancing will probably work well for you. Anyone who is sociable and can easily communicate with other people will excel at freelance work. Sometimes the hardest part is convincing a client to bid on you for a job or just speaking with them about the semantics of a particular job. People who are skilled but can't seem to find work that's stable are prime candidates for freelance work; it allows them to stay on top of their field without having to look for committed, full-time work.

Who Freelance Doesn't Work For

As I've stated previously, freelancing is not for everyone. If you're the type of person who loves to do the exact same thing every day then freelancing is probably not for you. Freelancing means you're dealing with many different clients who all have very different goals; if you're the type of person who keeps to a tight schedule and plans out the entire day the night before then freelance work may be too unpredictable for you. You might consider picking one day of the week to work on small freelance projects so you can supplement your existing income without throwing your schedule off balance. This problem can be drastically reduced if you develop a faithful client base that has consistent needs.

HOW DO I GET STARTED?

A lot of people are apprehensive about starting a freelance career. There are a thousand questions to ask because it's so incredibly different from having a traditional job. The first thing to do is to establish the difference between working freelance and owning your own business.

When you do freelance work you essentially are your own business. You have to pay taxes differently and you have to take care of the portion that would normally be covered by the company. That being said, there's a clear difference between being a freelancer and a business owner. Owning your own business means that you have an establishment or work from your home and you do business with clients, so far it's the same as freelancing. The difference is that businesses usually require a business license and special tax status. Aside from that, as a business you'll generally be the type of person who hires employees to get work done. The key difference is that if you own a business you usually sell a product or offer a standardized service and there are rarely contracts involved beyond the standard warrantees and terms of service etc. As a freelancer you are merely completing a service for a client and do contracts on a per-client basis; every situation is different.

It's a fine line but the point I'm trying to make is that freelance work is less complicated, less expensive and usually less work than owning your own business. As long as you set up an easy way to do your taxes (usually quarterly) you pretty much just have to get clients, do work and receive payment. Every country, state and territory is different but in general you don't require a special license to become a freelancer.

Who Makes The Money?

You might be wondering just who exactly makes all the money when it comes to freelancing. The best part of freelancing is that there is a niche for almost every skill. As long as you are proficient in a particular skill you have just as good a chance as anyone else of making a lot of money with freelance work. If you are good the demands upon your skills will be greater than the supply you can produce. Don't worry if you're not 100% sure about what your path is going to be. Throughout the course of this book we're going to assess what your strengths are and talk about how you can use them to their fullest for the best profit potential.

Why is freelancing so lucrative? Well as I said before, companies are outsourcing more and more work every year. It is much more cost effective for a company to outsource work to a free agent than to pay and maintain one full time employee. A company can find the right professional for a particular project rather than relying on a few employees who may not have the expertise needed to complete the project.

The people who make the most money doing freelance work are the type of people who know how to market themselves. They develop relationships with a large client base and know how to expand their business and maintain a certain level of quality. Many freelancers become extremely wealthy; in the end it all boils down to your client connections and your reputation. Who are these freelancers? How do they become rich? How do they find their clients?

You're probably excited to get going and start learning all of these fantastic techniques right now; not to worry, we'll be discussing all of these things and more in the coming chapters. The immediate answer is technology. The days of typewriters are gone. The days of waiting for a response from a client by postal service are gone. We live in a world of modern technology. Documents can be written, saved, and transmitted over thousands of miles in just a few short seconds. Words can reach thousands of people instantly. There is email now. In fact, you can chat online with clients on a real time basis. Information is easy to find, store, and send. That is why you can live anywhere you like as a freelancer. You are not confined to any one geographical address as long as some type of internet access is available.

Another advantage of modern technology is the ability for freelancers and their clients to find one another. There are many websites where a client can post a job and a freelancer can instantly respond to it. Again, geographical distance is not an issue. A client can be in Japan and the freelancer can be in sunny Florida and they can have a successful partnership agreement. Technology is the absolute answer to world-wide connections and limitless opportunity. Our ability to communicate with almost no restrictions allows a freelancer to connect with clients and complete projects from literally anywhere on the planet. Since your work is not necessarily localized, as it is with many businesses, you have limitless opportunities for wealth.

What's My Niche?

In case you're not familiar with the term, a niche is a specific or distinct segment of a market. This could be a particular category of work or a target audience. Work-At-Home Moms, for instance, is a particular niche. There are people all over the world who market products towards mothers who make a living from home. Alternatively there are millions of moms who work for themselves.

Another word you could use is penchant. People often say "I have a penchant for …" when they're talking about a particular strength or affinity to something. So your penchant is the strength that you have to market and your niche is the actual market you're going after. When it comes to freelance there really are no limits. You can do work for any niche imaginable. In the world of computers and technology the most common niches to work for are digitally based industries where the distance between client and freelancer has no bearing and work can be submitted on the internet instead of inperson. Here's a brief list of the most popular niches.

Writing

This could include just about anything. Writing is one of the most popular niche markets for freelancers because companies  everywhere need copy to be written but more often than not they don't really need so much that they can justify hiring a professional copywriter. The great thing about this market is that it's probably the most versatile one there is; as long as you are a competent writer you can write about any subject imaginable.

Voice-Over Work

This is another excellent niche. Like writing, this really requires no extra skills or knowledge beyond being able to read well. Even if you don't think you have a very good voice, you can become a successful voice.

It's how you say the words that matters.

Video and Screen Capture Video

A lot of large companies do training courses on an annual or semiannual basis. Especially if they're a computer-based company they will need screen capture video to train their employees on how to use essential software. Since these types of projects come up so rarely it's almost never necessary to hire an employee to make the videos so this is a popular niche to get freelance work in.

Research

Research is a lucrative freelancing option to get into although it's arguably hard to find reputable companies to work for. Research is exactly what it sounds like; you get small projects where you simply have to research a topic and provide information on it. It's rarely needed as much as other niches like writing but it's something to consider.

Help Desk Management

This is a lot easier than it sounds. Millions of websites that sell products and services have what's called a help desk. It's basically an online ticket system for customers to submit their problems and issues and then hopefully get them resolved. Most of your activities will include answering e-mails, submitting refunds and giving low-level support for products. For a large company this is usually something that full or part-time employees are hired for but sometimes when a company does a big launch it will hire freelancers to deal with a significant influx of support requests after a product launch.

Translation

If you know more than one language then your job opportunities are vastly expanded. There are a myriad of free translation programs on the web but most companies will want what's called a "Human" translation. This is exactly what it sounds like: a translation done by a human and not software. The reason this method is preferred is because the translations are usually more accurate and use colloquialisms and idioms that only a native speaker would think to use. Your tasks will usually include translating books, websites and manuals.

Graphic Design and Art

Despite the very specific, very talent-based nature of this niche it's one of the absolute most popular niches in regards to freelance work. Companies very rarely hire full-time or part-time graphic designers unless the company is involved with printing services etc. Almost all companies employ freelance graphic designers whenever they need to design new graphics or update old graphics; this can be anything from billboards to website images. If you have a talent for designing and creating images with the computer (and even better if you have an art degree) you can make a substantial profit from freelancing in the graphic design field.

Software Development and Programming

This is another very skill-based niche but it's also very lucrative.

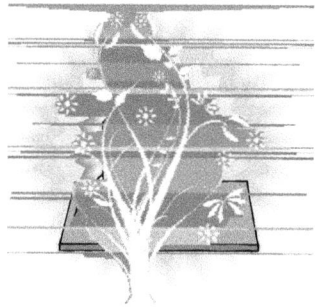

Again, most companies that need this type of work don't need it on a day-to-day basis so it's almost always hired out to freelancers. That means you'll have a much easier time finding a job than some other niches with more competition. The other benefit of freelance programming is that often times your clients will know absolutely nothing about programming so if you're skilled but can't quite cut it in the professional realm of programming you might still have a chance to build up your experience with freelance jobs.

Finance & Bookkeeping

You might be noticing a trend with the jobs I'm listing. The types of freelancers do are generally things that simply aren't required year-round.

Financing and accounting are things that people tend to

do periodically so they often hire a freelancer since it's way more cost effective than hiring an employee. The higher your education is the better but if you have experience with accounting you can still do well in this field without specific training.

That's just a tiny list of some of the most popular types of jobs, and even at that it's hardly complete. The possibilities are really limitless; I could probably fill the rest of this entire book just with job descriptions. Instead I'll give you a short list of some of the other types of jobs you might look into, aside from the 8 I mentioned earlier these are the most popular and highest paying freelance jobs:

- Animators (for film)
- Cartographers
- Computer programmers
- Consultants (political, architectural, sales, marketing, etc.)
- Culinary jobs (chefs, wine connoisseurs, etc.)
- Data encoders/Data processors
- Editors/Copyeditors
- Engineers
- Events planners (corporate planning, party planning, etc.)

- Financial planners
- Florists
- Inspectors
- Interior designers
- Landscape artists
- Massage therapists
- Photographers
- Private investigators
- Seamstresses
- Telemarketers
- Translators and interpreters
- Tutors
- Upholsterers
- Web designers

And there are many, many more where that came from. So, as you can see, as long as you're very good at *something*, there is a niche and a client base waiting for you to take their money!

Have a Plan!

Anyone who ever had a prosperous and profitable career as a freelancer didn't just jump into it with their eyes closed. You definitely don't want to just quite your day job and try to freelance or drop everything you're doing for it. You need to have a long-term plan that you can slowly execute and eventually reap the profits from.

You've already got a head start because you're reading this book. The next step is to do some extra research outside of this text in order to assess where your opportunities lie and how deep you can get into freelancing at this point.

For instance, if you already have a job but simply aren't making enough money, you can try freelancing on your spare time to try and supplement your income. If you find that your freelance jobs are slowly increasing and beginning to pay more than your day job you can consider quitting and asking for a part-time schedule and focusing on your freelance work. Any transition you make should be slow; until you get established as a freelancer with a decent client base it's just as volatile as the employment job market; the only difference is that finding new clients is a lot easier than finding new employers.

The first bit of research you should do is with online freelancing services. Luckily for you there are tons. Once you've used one or two of these services a while you can eventually start running the whole show yourself but these networks are a great place to get into freelancing because they do a lot of the work for you. After you've become an established freelancer with a client base you can move past these websites and make slightly higher profits. These are my top picks for freelancing websites:

- Allfreelance.com
- Aquent.com
- Elance.com
- Craigslist.org
- vWorker.com
- Ifreelance.com
- Odesk.com
- Centralmall.com
- Consultingexchange.com
- Contentexchange.com
- Ework.com
- freelanceworkexchange.com
- Freelancejobsearch
- Guru.com
- Monster.com
- Sologig.com

Of these websites I'm going to specifically talk about ODesk, Craigslist, Elance, vWorker (formerly rent-a-coder) and Guru. These are my 5 favorite websites to use and they all have unique advantages that make each of them worth trying out.

How these sites works varies pretty widely. Some sites, like Craigslist, are more so bulletin boards than networks. Other sites charge you a monthly or yearly fee but most of them will offer a free service in addition to their paid service (or they'll take a percentage of your profits). Look around and see if your skills match with any of the jobs posted. Even if you don't see many jobs requiring your skills, don't give up. It could mean that your niche is in an untapped area. If so, Congratulations! This means that you will have a lot less competition.

Look for a variety of jobs that match your skills. When you find some, look at how much those jobs pay - the amounts will vary. As clients become more familiar with your work and you build trust and a reputation, you can begin to demand more money.

Many sites require you to bid on projects. The stipulation is that you have to pay some sort of commission to the company who owns the site. Take some time and look at these sites. You may also use a search engine such as Google and use the key word "freelance" or you may add some specific skills to narrow your search such as "freelance writing."

Before we move on I'm going to give you an overview of my top three websites so you can get an idea of how they work. These include vWorker, Elance and Craigslist.

ONLINE FREELANCE & SUBCONTRACTING

The Internet is quite possibly the most powerful communication tool on the planet right now. For millions of people, the internet has become a medium that allows for freelancing opportunities that were impossible just a few decades ago. Freelancing on the internet has become a dependable source of income for many people, especially for skilled professionals from countries where jobs are scarce and salaries are low by international standards.

If I had to pinpoint the start of the "E-Lancing" boom I guess it would probably sometime in the early 90's. Computers and even the Internet had existed before then but until the release of the major personal computer operating systems like Windows 95, marketing on the Internet had not become ubiquitous. During this time in the U.S. software companies realized that they could save a lot of money by hiring overseas programmers who would work for less. These developers and programmers were well-versed in web design, application and database development, as well as system administration.

 Studies have shown that 1 out of every 5 contracted websites, software development, and graphic designs worldwide, are the products of outsourcing to freelancers. Beyond software requirements, internet freelancing now involves such services as design (graphic design, logos, brochures, illustrations, etc.), writing (advertising copywriting, web content, creative writing and ghostwriting), business consulting (competitive analysis, marketing planning, accounting and bookkeeping, email management and direct marketing) legal services, administrative support, engineering, architecture and a host of audio, video, and multimedia services and applications.

Today there are many online marketplaces where buyers and sellers of such services meet and do business. These websites provide a forum where buyers can post their job requirements and qualified coders can submit proposals for these jobs. Based on these proposals, the buyer chooses who they believe to be the most qualified for the job and awards that job to them. Once the selected coder completes the job the buyer sends payment to the online marketplace. The online market place deducts its fee and sends the rest to the coder.

If the coder lives in a country where jobs are hard to find or where salaries are low, they have the potential benefit of earning US dollars. Perhaps the best thing about earning money in this manner is that they do not have to leave their country or even the comfort of their own home.

The buyer benefits as well. They are able to get the job done in a professional manner at a relatively low cost. With this kind of win-win situation, it is no surprise why the online outsourcing industry has become a flourishing business. And with the presence of escrow services on many of these websites, the element of fraud is taken out of the equation and coders are assured of collecting their fees. Such is the beauty of online freelancing.

Subcontracting

With the success of the freelancing business on the internet, a new type of business opportunity has risen for the more enterprising coders. It is called subcontracting. That means getting freelance jobs on the internet and subcontracting them to other coders at a profit.

Subcontracting is ideal for coders who are not just technical people but who have a keen business sense as well. These are people who can immediately gauge which projects can be easily subcontracted out but still bear them a profit.

To succeed here, you have to be a skilled communicator with good people skills. You also have to be an expert in the type of work which you are subcontracting.

Do you think you may have the skills necessary to contract out these kinds of jobs? There are three basic elements that you, as a coder, must know in order to subcontract out jobs effectively:

1. Technical skills

I've said it before and I'll say it again: You need to have the technical skills to do any job that you accept - even if, and especially, if you subcontract that job. You should not only be well-versed but an expert in your chosen field of endeavor. You have to be able to verify the quality of the work and be able to do it yourself if something happens and your subcontractor can't finish the job.

A. Quality Control

You have to make sure that the work you receive from subcontractors is the kind of quality that the buyer will accept. Ideally, the quality should be better than the buyers lowest accepted standard.

You cannot get paid on a regular basis if the quality of work your subcontractor coder submits is below standard. While most buyers will understand missing the deadline by a few hours or a day, virtually none of them will tolerate poor quality. Yes, sometimes they are paying rock-bottom rates based on the business standards of developed nations, but it is still a professional transaction between buyers and coders and, as such, they expect professional work.

If the job you are subcontracting involves writing you need to be a good writer too. You will need to have impeccable grammar and the ability to communicate clearly. In addition, you will also need to know how to edit for clarity and brevity. You will have to possess the talent needed to improve the subcontractors work so that it is worth more in the eyes of your buyers.

B. Pick up the Slack

There will be occasions (and hopefully not many of them) when one of your coders will be unable to complete a job that has been awarded to you from a buyer. Or you may have landed a job and can't find any qualified coder to subcontract it to. Given the short notice and the difficulty of finding a good coder, you may have to roll up your sleeves and do the job yourself. It pays to have the talent and technical skills to do so.

Beyond the ability to add to the number of articles and words required, you may also have to redo the writing in terms of the quality required. Let's say one of your coders has impeccable grammar but a style that is dry and long-winded. That may not be what the buyer expects and you, as the main contact, will have to do something to fix that. If you have an elegant sense of style and a way of making words come to life, then you have the skills to put an extra dash of flavor into the work.

In the minds of many, talent is the most important benefit that an online entrepreneur must have if they are going to be successful using subcontractors.

2. Get into a Freelancer Network

To subcontract jobs, you will naturally need to have access to skilled freelancers. The key word here is "skilled." It is easy enough to bring together a group of online workers who have technical knowledge in a given area but are their skills adequate in the world market? Once again, having an eye for talent comes into play.

The good news is that it is easy to find skilled freelancers.

Freelancers who hire subcontractors can often find freelancer support from the same place where they landed the online job in the first place. These freelancers, originally providers of services, switch profiles to become buyers of services. They look for freelancers who have the same skills they do except that these freelancers are willing to work for less.

Two good sources of this kind of skilled freelancer can be found at vWorker.com and Elance.com. which were profiled earlier?

In addition, the internet is not the only place to find your skilled freelancers either. Perhaps all you may have to do is take a good look around you.

For example, there is a skilled journalist from Manila in the Philippines who has been a successful freelancer for years. He recently started outsourcing some of the jobs he has landed online and has been rather successful at it. Since he works in a newspaper, he simply passes on some of the work to his colleagues in the press. Since his colleagues are all professional writers who have established their own credibility, he has no problem delivering quality work or meeting deadlines.

However, this kind of approach will not work for everyone. Perhaps the biggest reason why he succeeds is the low wages even highly skilled professionals receive in the Philippines.

Today, through subcontracting jobs instead of doing them himself, he has been able to increase his monthly income threefold.

3. It's All About Business Sense

Getting the jobs and subcontracting them to other freelancers is a profitable endeavor but one that's not explicitly simple. The only way to become a truly successful entrepreneur, however, is to have a good sense of business.

In subcontracting you basically become the third party in that you act as a middle man (or woman) between the client and the worker. It's a little complicated because you communicate with the initial buyer and the primary seller but you, yourself, are also a buyer and seller. A simple way to think of it is to take the other seller out of the picture. You and the buyer have a client/seller relationship and you happen to be outsourcing your work - end of story. The trick here is that the profits you make from the client's purchase must exceed the cost of your outsourced work. So, like any market, you must sell *your* services high and buy the outsourcer's services *low.*

Do you think you have the key qualities necessary to succeed in outsourcing work to subcontractors? If you think you do, why not try it?

The following are a few key considerations that will help you successfully launch your new career:

A. Carefully and Clearly Define the Scope of the Project

The first thing you should do before accepting a single project is carefully consider your skills and talents. Ask yourself, "What can I do that is easily marketable?" Determine the areas that you are most confident about in your work and decide if you have the skills necessary to differentiate between subpar work and excellent work. Assess yourself with as little bias as possible and be honest with yourself.

The one thing you usually don't' want to do is try and do a hundred different things at once. Have you ever heard the phrase, "Jack of all trades, master of none?" That last little part is what will get you. Clients higher freelancers with a specific skillset because they want the person who is the absolute best at that one thing. Expanding your niche in too many directions won't nab you any extra clients if you don't appeal as an authority in your field. It might be a way to make a few extra bucks in the short term but it's a sure-fire way of ruining your reputation in the long run.

Just imagine what it would mean to your reputation if your outsourced freelancers were submitting inferior work to you and you did not know how to tell the difference. You may get away with submitting this kind of work to buyers and they may not raise a howl given that the work meets their bare minimum, but more than likely they will never use your services again. Sooner or later word will spread about your penchant for delivering inferior products and no one may want to hire you.

Defining your scope of work is also practical because it allows you to concentrate your efforts in that area alone. This will dramatically increase your efficiency and allow you to gain a reputation much faster.

In business school, professors teach students to avoid working on several small business projects at the same time because chances are a small business project will take almost as much effort and time to become profitable as a large one. Instead students are counseled to take on the largest project available and focus their energies on that alone. Hopefully, you can do the same.

B. Carefully Choose Your Projects

Any experienced online entrepreneur should understand and know how to gage his or her profit margin. It's essential to accurately assess how much you need to bid to land a project and how much it will cost to bid it out.

Before you begin to bid for a project, you should have an idea of how much you will potentially earn from it. Those valuations should become second nature to you. You know that Project X costs $200 and Project Y costs $300 and you know you can find subcontractors who can finish the work for $100 and $150, respectively.

Aside from the quality of the project you also have to understand the importance of meeting the deadline. The best jobs for this kind of set-up are naturally those which have the longest deadlines. It is important to be able to estimate how long the job will actually take

When it comes to meeting deadlines, one way to manage your timetable effectively is to divide the large jobs and farm them out to several coders.

Let's say you've been awarded a writing job to write an e-book on childcare with 10 chapters for $2,000 over a 45 day period of time. Bid out each chapter separately among 10 coders and allocate, say, $100 for each chapter over a 25 day period. This way you don't have to worry about the deadline because you've given yourself a 20-day buffer and you stand to earn $1,000 for your efforts.

If you are going to handle a project in this manner you must be able to rewrite the articles you receive in order to make sure the entire book "flows" seamlessly and that the same style and tone of voice is consistent throughout.

A. Cultivate a strong talent pool

In many cases, this is the most important asset needed when subcontracting work to others. Here are a few additional tips to help you out in this regard:

1 Know how to hire a good coder

There are four things you should look at when hiring a coder – their resume, their samples, their rating, and their client testimonials.

The last two are critical because it is easy to prepare a bogus resume and samples, especially on the internet.

If you look at those four things and feel you have found the person you are looking for, hire them.

2 Know how to keep them happy

A happy coder always delivers better work than an unhappy one, given the same skill level. You keep your coders happy by dealing in a polite and professional manner, paying them on time and understanding them when they fall or falter (and believe me, they will miss a deadline now and then). Give them respect and they will give you their best.

4. Take Care of Your Clients

Here is the main reason why quality counts – it is quality, more than anything else, that will make your customers come running back to you again and again. Always put a premium on quality. First-class work is sometimes hard to find, especially given a limited budget. If you consistently deliver first-class work, you assure yourself and your coders of a prosperous business well into the future.

There is a popular saying in sales which says that "It is eight times easier to get new business from your current clients than it is from cold calls." In other words, make sure you ask your clients for referrals from people they know or work with who may need the service you provide.

Some coders hesitate when it comes to asking for referrals because they feel it is unprofessional. They feel asking for referrals is like asking for a favor. That is not really the case. If you have faith in your ability to deliver good work you are actually helping your client because of your willingness to provide quality work to their friends or business associates. That will reflect well on them too. It is a two-way street.

Now that we have looked at three on line venues we are ready to look at developing eye catching resumes that will help you land some of those great paying opportunities.

FREELANCING WEBSITES

1. vWorker (AKA RentACoder)

vWorker, formerly known as RentACoder, is a place where software buyers and software coders meet to do business. Doing business in vWorker is extremely simple. Clients (aka buyers) post their requirements on the site and coders (aka programmers and writers) make a bid for these requirements. The buyer hires the coder who they feel is best qualified and pays them when the job is completed. Pretty easy right?

vWorker is pretty much an online market where companies and individuals with programming and coding needs find qualified programmers to write code for them. It provides excellent opportunities for software programmers and freelance writers to put their hard-earned skills to use and earn cash. One of the marvelous things about this site is that writers can actually find work and get paid without ever leaving the comfort of their home. And with vWorker's "Safe Project Escrow" (see below), coders can work on projects without the stress of worrying about the agreed-on payment time.

2. Who are the people on vWorker?

vWorker has a vast international community of buyers and coders spanning virtually every continent in the world. They have over 64,700 buyers registered on the site as well as a pool of over 159,000 registered coders. At any given time, vWorker has over 2,000 open bid requests awaiting qualified coders.

There is a world of opportunities available through vWorker.

vWorker was founded and is owned by Ian Ippolito. He is the Chief Executive Officer and holds a bachelor's degree in computer science from the University of Central Florida. The offices are located in Tampa, Florida, USA.

3. What Are the Profit Possibilities?

Fees vary depending on the nature and scope of the particular project. The smaller jobs can cost $20 or less while the larger jobs can pay you thousands of dollars. The sky is the limit in vWorker. You get paid according to your skill level and your capacity and readiness to work hard and deliver the goods on time.

4. What is the Method of Payment?

One of the best things about vWorker is that they take care of the money side of your business transactions with buyers. They have a marvelous instrument called "Safe Project Escrow" which assures coders that they will be paid. Here is how it works: Let's say a buyer selects your bid from the dozens of bids received. After approving your bid, the buyer puts the agreed upon amount in escrow, meaning the funds are automatically forwarded to the vWorker website. Once your work is complete and the buyer approves and accepts it, the funds are released to you.

Your accumulated earnings on vWorker can be released to you on the 15th of each month, at the end of each month or both times.

Payment is usually sent a few days (two or three) after your selected payment period. There are three payment options on vWorker:

1. Snail Mail Check
2. Western Union
3. Pay Pal

If you're doing a large job that's over $100-$200 per pay period then I suggest the first two options and here's why: PayPal can and will hold your money for up to 6 months and more often than not they won't even provide you with a reason. PayPal is extremely convenient and safe; that's why millions of people use it today. That being said, PayPal is infamous for holding funds for up to 6 months at the slightest sign of a breach in contract. Even if PayPal is mistaken that will hold your money and will not provide you with any restitution for having to wait 6 months for it.

In order for the website to be maintained, vWorker charges a 15% fee on a coder's income. This is automatically deducted before payment is sent to the coder. This 15% can actually be reduced depending on the auction type (see below) and the payment method that the coder and buyer agree upon.

5. How do I get jobs?

There are two basic ways to get jobs at vWorker:

E. By winning bid requests – Once a bid request is placed on the site, virtually anyone can make a bid on that particular project. From the dozen or so bids received, the buyer selects one and that winning bidder gets the job.

F. Private Auctions – These are auctions where you are invited to participate as opposed to the first one where you make a bid on a project that is open to all. In private auctions you either have a satisfied customer who asks you to do a new job or a new customer who is impressed with your rating and decides to invite you to bid on their job.

6. How can I improve my chances of getting future work?

A. **Focus On Your Resume**

When you sign up to vWorker, there is a portion in the sign-up procedure that asks for your resume. Unfortunately, a lot of newcomers do not give enough attention to their resume. This is a major mistake. At the beginning and with no track record on the site whatsoever, your resume is one of the few things that buyers can study to assess your capability to do their job. For this reason, it is of paramount importance that you are able to present yourself competently on your resume. For detailed information on how to do your resume see Chapter 3.

When writing your resume, you should remember to be clear and concise. After all, you are a writer and clarity and brevity should be two of your strongest points. Don't simply put down a laundry list of past positions and tasks you have handled in your career. Give brief descriptions to each of them, particularly about the writing aspect of that particular job.

If your resume is too long, chances are it may turn off prospective buyers and limit your chances of landing jobs. The best advice is to include only your past professional experiences that relate to the current position you are seeking in vWorker.

B. Intrigue with a Creative Bid Letter

Every time you make a bid for a project, you will have to write a bid letter. Make sure the first line in the bid letter catches the attention of the buyer. Make it lucrative and interesting. If you are a writer you already know this is called the "hook". It is what can make the difference between a buyer paying attention to you or just passing you by as ordinary. It is an ideal opportunity to show off your skills as a writer. Your letter should tell the buyer one important thing: why you are an excellent candidate, if not the best person, for this particular job.

Remember, the ideal bid letter should discuss your experience and expertise. It should contain references to past jobs or writing assignments that are related to the job you are bidding for. If there is nothing in your work history that is related to the current job then emphasize your ability to handle a wide array of different subjects and your capacity to learn fast.

Another thing that buyers look for is speed and efficiency. Let the buyer know that you can tackle their particular job efficiently and quickly. Give them a firm commitment about meeting the deadline and assure them that you will be communicating with them regularly in the course of the job, if only to give them updates.

C. **Only Send Your Best Work**

Although not every buyer requires coders to send samples when they bid for a project, it is always best to send them samples anyway. Your samples will give buyers an idea of how you write and whether your particular style fits their project. For this reason, it is best to provide samples that have the same subject matter or are at least related to the subject matter of the job you are bidding on. This way, you not only exhibit your writing style but impress upon the buyer your familiarity with the subject. This is always a major plus. However, if you have no related previous work, it does not have to mean you will be overlooked for the job. Send your best samples and you may have chance of landing that job anyway.

D. **Start Slowly and Build Up**

The most difficult time to get jobs on vWorker is at the beginning when you are new to the site. That is because you are an unknown entity, with no track record on vWorker whatsoever. You may have a glowing resume and impressive samples, but many coders want to know how you work given the parameters and conditions of vWorker. For this reason your first priority should be getting a few jobs under your belt. Don't disregard the small projects (small pay, small deliverables, etc.). You may also bid for the major projects but, as a newbie, your chances of getting the smaller jobs are better.

Initially, your objective will be to establish a track record. Start with some simple projects that you can do easily. Don't make the size of the payment a priority. In fact, you will be much better off if you don't pay any attention to the payment at all. Once you have a number of projects under your belt – and potential buyers will take note of that – they are more likely to regard you favorably because you have a history of delivering the goods.

Of course, if you are a very talented writer with outstanding credentials and excellent samples, then, by all means, go for the higher paying jobs. There are always exceptions to the rule.

E. **Keep an Eye on Quality**

In every job you do always give the buyer your best work. There are two reasons for this. First, you make the buyer happy and increase the likelihood that they will use you again for future projects. Second, the buyer will give you a good rating after completing the job. On vWorker, a coder's rating is one of the main factors that buyers consider when handing out jobs.

Quality work ensures a satisfied customer. And satisfied customers give coders perfect "10" ratings. That is the highest rating you can get on vWorker. If you can establish a string of a dozen or so consecutive 10 ratings, then you are sending a clear signal to all potential customers that you can do an excellent job for them. This will greatly enhance your ability to get more jobs.

F. Build up Your Reputation

Aside from ratings; buyers also post comments on their coder's work after they have completed the job. These comments are another thing that buyers look at since they convey much more than what a numerical rating can say. For instance, getting a 10 rating will tell prospective clients that you have satisfied your previous customers but the comments portion is where they will learn about your professionalism, attitude and working style. Comments are usually short one-liners that summarize a coder's performance. They may say things like, "It was a pleasure to work with a real pro like him" or "She delivered on all her promises and provided excellent results." These are the kinds of comments that can weigh heavily on a buyer's decision making process when looking for the right coder for the job.

G. Be Adaptable

Since the projects on vWorker run the gamut of practically any subject imaginable, it always pays to exhibit versatility to prospective buyers. Show them you can successfully write about a wide range of topics and that you can adapt different writing styles be it serious, humorous, or provocative.

Among the most popular topics for writers on vWorker are travel, health, real estate, relationships, romance, technology, the internet, and similar subjects. It pays to have some knowledge about these subjects tucked under your belt.

H. Take Deadlines Seriously

Most of the buyers on vWorker have deadlines and they expect the coders they hire to deliver the work within the agreed-on deadline. This is a basic requirement for any professional writer. Deadlines have to be regarded as almost sacred. No one wants to hire an undependable writer. If you want to be regarded as a professional and paid like a professional, you have to act like a professional and meeting your deadlines is part of that package.

I. Update Clients on a Regular Basis

In line with being a professional, freelance writers must also give their clients regular updates about how the work is progressing. Buyers will always want to know where their project stands. Most of the time, they just need to know that the writing is going smoothly and that you, the writer, will have no trouble meeting the deadline. However, they also want to know about any problems you may encounter, especially if these problems will hamper you from meeting the deadline or delivering quality work.

Thankfully, in vWorker, there is a built-in mechanism that reminds coders that they haven't given an update in three days. Once you receive that notice, you know it is time to give your buyer an update. In addition, for major projects spanning weeks of work and costing hundreds, maybe thousands, of dollars, coders are required to give the buyer an update every Friday. vWorker moderators can penalize the coder if they fail to do so. This will definitely affect their overall rating.

J. Don't Be Stubborn

Let's say you have just completed a batch of 20 difficult articles and have barely beaten the week-long deadline set by your buyer. You heave a sigh of relief and thank your lucky stars that the work is finished. That, however, is not the case. The work is not officially finished until the buyer formally accepts it. If the buyer is unhappy with the work, they have every right to request that you make revisions (as long as these are reasonable) and you are obliged to comply.

Unfortunately, many writers resist making revisions by insisting they have met every requirement stated in the buyer's original bid. They may be right and they may even convince the buyer that they are right. But if the buyer is forced to accept the work, the coder may suffer the consequences of refusing to respect the buyers request for a revision. The buyer may "punish" the coder by giving them a poor rating or by posting unflattering, nasty comments that will certainly affect the coder's future prospects of getting jobs with other buyers.

K. **Honest Really is the Best Policy**

As a professional writer, never assume to know what the buyer wants if you are unsure about it. If you are not clear about something, ask. Don't go ahead and write about something if you are not absolutely sure about what your buyer expects. If you do and you are wrong, the buyer may ask you to rewrite the project all over again. This is something that all writers absolutely hate to do, correct? Hence, make it a rule to never assume. Buyers won't mind if you ask them a lot of questions as long as these questions can help you deliver the kind of high quality work that they demand.

L. **Make suggestions**

Most clients will appreciate some suggestions here and there. This lets them know that you are taking their project seriously and paying attention to your work. It's also good to try and put out the best work possible if you're going to use anything as examples for your resume and portfolio; clients don't always make the best decisions so trying to make them lean towards more sensible ones usually doesn't hurt.

M. **Go Above and Beyond**

This is a general rule for success in virtually every human endeavor. Go the extra mile and deliver more than what is expected. This does not mean writing more articles than the buyer wants. What it does mean is proofreading your work and putting in the extra time it takes to make necessary revisions. Do everything you can to insure that the work you submit is impeccable and represents your best work.

E-Lance

Elance is widely regarded as one of the largest online marketplace in the world for a host of professional services, especially those involving creativity and technology-based endeavors. It is a popular outsourcing venue for many small and medium-size businesses that wish to make significant savings by bidding out their projects to qualified professionals and service providers all around the world. For highly-skilled and qualified professionals, Elance provides a tremendous opportunity to earn dollars right in the comfort of their own homes.

1. The Signup Process

Like most of these websites, signing up for Elance is pretty simple and straightforward. Here are some tips for signing up with this particular freelance website:

1. Click the "Join Now" button on the upper left-hand side of the site.

2. In the Select Category page, click the box that applies to your specialty. Click "Continue".

3. You have four options at the Choose a Membership Program page:

    A. Select Membership - $149 quarterly

    B. Professional Membership - $69.00 quarterly

    C. Limited Membership - $22.00 quarterly

    D. Courtesy Listing - FREE

(A detailed discussion of each membership level can be found below.)

Pick the one that is right for you. Select Membership is ideal for agencies or businesses. General freelancers and individuals will likely choose from either Professional

Membership, which is ideal for individual professionals; Limited Membership, which is ideal for those who wish to place limited project bids; and Courtesy Listing, which is ideal for simply posting a provider profile (you wait for clients to contact you and will not be allowed to place bids).

In this page, you must also select a category. For example, if you are exclusively a voice actor then select "Voice Talent." Other options include Animation, Commercials, Embedded Video/Audio, Music, and Others - Multimedia Services, Photography & Editing,

Podcasts, Radio Ads & Jingles, Videography & Editing and Viral Videos.

4. Fill-in your contact information and press "continue." Wait for your confirmation then press "Go" to complete the rest of the sign-up process.

5. In the Seller Profile page, select the subcategories where you wish to display your profile. The number of sub-categories you can select varies depending on the type of member you are. For example, Courtesy Members can only choose up to three sub-categories. Bear in mind that you can only bid on projects in those subcategories where your profile is displayed. Once you've made your selections, press "Done."

6. Click on the portion that says, "You must describe the services you offer to complete your profile." Fill in the requested information. Once you're done, click "Update Profile." A preview of how your profile will appear to others is presented to you. Now you have successfully signed in.

2. The Benefits of Having a Membership

Elance has four basic membership benefits that are available to all members (including courtesy listings) regardless of level. They are as follows:

1. Your profile is posted on the Elance website and it gives out vital details to prospective clients

2. Your portfolio is also posted and it contains samples of your finest work

3. You get regular notifications on new projects in the categories that you are interested in

4. You may receive invitations from interested buyers who want you to bid on their projects

Professional and Limited members get additional benefits that are not available to Courtesy Members such as the following:

1. Participation in Elance's packaged service program, which is by invitation only

2. A bid allotment of $80 per month

3. A private workspace for easier communication with prospective and present clients

4. Assistance from Elance in billing and payment matters

5. Inclusion in the Elance rating system, which grades various members on the quality of work they deliver and on their qualifications for particular jobs. Customers use these ratings as a gauge for a member's ability to complete the job at hand.

6. In case of disputes with clients, members receive assistance from Elance in mediation and investigation

7. Availability of the Elance escrow service to ensure that all payments are made in a timely manner

3. Project Acquisition

Once you have completed your service provider profile, you can start getting projects. There are two basic ways you can land a project:

1. Bid for a project in the project marketplace. If the client finds your particular bid the most appealing, the job will be awarded to you.

2. You are invited to bid on a project. This usually happens when a previous client was happy with your work and wants to work with you again. It also happens when a new client finds your profile and/or samples appealing and wants to give you a chance.

4. Tips on Getting Started

This section lists several helpful tips to get you started on the right foot. It is critical that you have the right mind-set for the challenges that lay ahead. Bear in mind that the biggest challenge to success on Elance comes at the beginning when you have no track record, rating or reputation. Do not be discouraged if you fail to get a project right away. Stick in there and try to follow these pointers as well as you can. Remember that worthwhile things seldom come easy.

A few important tips on getting started:

1. Examine your Experience and Skill

All members are required to sign up at Elance. Putting the right information in your member profile can be a give you the hiring edge over your competition.

Use this as an opportunity to put your best foot forward. List all your major work experience that is significant to the Elance category you have chosen. State the number of years you have been a voice talent and enumerate the most significant projects you have done. Make special note of the most challenging and impressive voice characters you have played.

Try to be clear and concise. Instead of just listing all your professional positions, focus on the depth and breadth of voice characterizations and personalities you have portrayed. Explain why you chose to act them out in a certain way. The more understanding you can give to your potential employer about the why's and how's of doing a project in a particular way, the better chance you will have of getting hired.

Remember, you can never land a job by drowning prospective employers under an avalanche of useless information. In fact, the exact opposite may be true – a long and wordy profile may rub prospective clients the wrong way so much so that they will remove you from their list of candidates.

2. Submit a Jaw-Dropping Proposal

To land a project, you have to submit a proposal that catches the attention of the project proponent. You can do this by putting the right kind of information in the two main fields that you have to fill in when making a proposal: "Ask the Buyer a Question" and "Describe Your Proposal".

Asking an intelligent question about the requirement can sometimes capture the customer's attention. It can tell him that you understand clearly the nature of the work involved and simply need some clarification. Questions that seek guidance about how to properly execute a script and what tone and personality to utilize (assuming that these are not obvious) are appreciated by clients because such queries reflect the voice talent's concern for meeting the client's needs and expectations. It shows you have enough insight about the requirement to know what to ask.

In the "Describe your Proposal" field, voice talents should impress upon the client that they understand what is needed. If you give information about a similar job that you have accomplished in the past and attach a sample of that to your proposal, then you have just increased your chances of getting that job.

Some projects have a script attached for voice talents to interpret and send as part of their proposal. In such cases, use the "Describe Your Proposal" field to explain why you read a particular sample script in a certain way and why you chose to project a certain mood or personality.

You should also mention that you will be more than happy to submit additional samples based on any new in-puts or guidelines that the client may have. This is especially effective in cases where the client likes your voice but is having second thoughts about your delivery. Providing additional samples that address those concerns may convince the client that you are the right person for the job.

When it comes to submitting proposals, do not submit a "generic" bid that does not specifically address the job requirement. Savvy customers can detect a generic proposal right away and just as quickly eliminate the guilty party from consideration.

3. Don't Waste Time with Subpar Samples

When uploading voice samples onto your portfolio, you should carefully scrutinize each piece of work. Only include those that you consider to be world class because these samples will be made available to prospective clients from all over the world.

If you are an amateur voice talent with no actual work experience yet, then you can produce your own samples. These voice samples are critical to your success so give them all the attention and time they deserve. Without job samples, any effort you exert to land a job is likely to be a waste of time.

Some projects provide scripts for talents to voice and send to the customer as a sample. These samples should be taken seriously. Tackle these samples the way you would tackle the actual job itself. These samples, more than anything else in the member's profile or proposal, will be the determining factor in deciding who to hire.

4. Impress Clients with Range

If you have the talent to execute scripts using different voices or a wide range of personalities, then do so. The more samples you provide, the greater your chances of landing the project. Of course, all of the samples you submit must be appropriate to the script and the client's particular needs.

5. Develop a Good Track Record

When searching for someone to hire, clients look at the number of jobs a member has already completed on the site and the ratings that member has received for those jobs. These are sign posts that tell clients about the competence and dependability of specific Elance members. They are key indicators of exactly how desirable a member's services can be.

For a member to be competitive on Elance, they must have an impressive track record of jobs completed and a glowing history of high ratings.

Neophyte Elance members should concentrate on building a track record and getting good ratings rather than earning the big bucks right away. A sound strategy for newcomers is to bid low for projects and sacrifice some income to ensure a better chance of landing jobs. A string of completed projects and high ratings increases a member's credentials tremendously in the Elance marketplace. It will greatly boost the chances of getting more work.

Naturally, there are exceptions to this rule. If you feel you qualify, then as by all means, go after the most lucrative projects on the site. Just remember that talent is not the whole picture. You also have to be diligent and disciplined enough to meet deadlines and consistently turn out the kind of quality work that the higher echelon of customer demands.

6. How To Get Stable, Regular Work

Now that you have learned the ropes of Elance and have notched a significant number of projects under your belt, there are two things to bear in mind for the sake of your future success.

1. **Keep Your Standards High**

The only sure way a voice talent can earn a regular and continuing income from Elance is to consistently deliver quality work.

Sustained excellence is hard to come by and highly coveted by clients no matter where in the world they are based. If you always deliver high quality work and leave your clients satisfied, then you can almost certainly count on repeat business coming your way.

In addition, a member who constantly delivers work of the highest standards is assured of having excellent reviews and ratings.

For an online marketplace that is as active and competitive as this one, a superlative rating is tantamount to winning half the battle.

2. **Maintain a Great Reputation**

Clearly, a good reputation is related to the above strategy of constantly delivering high quality work. However, it goes beyond just the actual work itself. A good reputation will assure you of winning the other half of the battle.

Cultivating a good reputation means never missing a deadline, being gracious and professional in all your dealings, and going the extra mile to make revisions or extra voice studies to meet your clients' demands. It means defusing potential disputes and handling every aspect of your job with diplomacy and professionalism.

A good reputation means you are a professional of the highest degree. Like scaling a mountain, it takes time and effort to reach the top. But once there, you will find that excellence is its own reward. If you can successfully maintain high standards, then you will be financially set for life.

Craigslist

Craigslist (www.craigslist.org) is one of the more unique options as far as online freelancing goes. Craigslist is not a traditional freelance website; it's essentially a bulletin board where people can post job listings or resume/CV information. The beauty of Craigslist is that it's area specific and has targeted categories that make it really easy to find exactly what you're looking for. Craigslist is also a free website; it costs nothing to sign up and post projects or contact posters about their projects. There's no commissions or extra fees of any kind.

The only caveat of this system is that you work with clients directly via e-mail or physical communication. Since Craigslist is only a bulletin board there are no guarantees of payment or security measures. For this reason it's always good to exercise a bit of caution when using craigslist. You're bound to discover job opportunities that you never would have found on other websites so it's definitely worth it; you just have to know how to be careful.

1. How to Post on Craigslist

I guess you could call this the easiest part. All you have to do is go to the website, choose the appropriate category and create a post. Here's a step-by-step guide:

1. Go to www.craigslist.org and select your region.
2. Select the category that applies to you. The categories that you'll mostly want to use are under **Services, Jobs** and **Gigs.**
3. Click on **[post]** in the upper right hand corner.
4. Select your appropriate category again.
5. You may have to sign up to post in certain categories. Simply click the link and then click the link on the following page that says **sign up for an account**.

Enter an e-mail address and fill out the rest of the information to sign up for your account. When you're done, log in to craigslist and repeat from step one.

6. Now you're taken to the actual posting window. Simply give your post a title, fill in a location (usually just the City) and then write your post.

Generally speaking you can treat it like a resume listing. You should give an explanation of your skills and proficiencies.

It's a good idea to use the anonymized e-mail option to prevent yourself from getting a lot of spam. You may still get spam but it will stop if you delete your craigslist post and the spammers won't have your e-mail address on file.

7. Click continue after you're happy with your post, verify that the post is correct and then click the submit button.

8. If you did not sign up you may have to activate your post by following a link in the e-mail that craigslist will send you.

9. Now your post is active. People can read your post and may respond to you via the e-mail address you provided.

2. General Tips for Using Craigslist

How to just essential so that you can determine what part of your skills you should market and how exactly you should go about marketing them. It's sort of a balancing act wherein you're constantly trying to find an area that's not being overworked and watch out for areas that are overworked. The key is to find a niche where the supply for skills is low but the demand is high.

HOW TO MARKET YOURSELF

The law of supply and demand affects much as freelancing just as it affects any other aspect of the economy. You can't succeed unless there's a market for the services  you have to offer. If the market just isn't there then you aren't going to make it. Research is essential so that you can determine what part of your skills you should market and how exactly you should go about marketing them. It's sort of a balancing act wherein you're constantly trying to find an area that's not being overworked and watch out for areas that are overworked. The key is to find a niche where the supply for skills is low but the demand is high.

One thing that freelancing might require of you is to go back to school. If the demand is too low or the supply too high for your current skill set, you can gain experience or education in order to fit into a niche where the demand is high and the supply is low. With experience and specialization your value as a freelancer increases.

So far you have discovered that having skills and identifying these skills is essential. Next you learned that finding a niche that is high in demand is important to success. What you need to understand now is that none of these will work if you don't also have passion for what you are doing. Your heart has to be in it. This is the fuel in the car that keeps you moving toward your goal.

Sometimes passion and skills are not enough. Let's say you are passionate about computer repair. In fact you are so passionate about it that you went to school to earn a degree in computer technology and repair. More than that, you graduated at the top of your class. You decide you want a job repairing PC's. The sad truth is that for every job available there are about 10 qualified people and about 30 unqualified people who are applying for it. Because the field is not as specialized as it once was and because there are so many more qualified people who can do PC repair, your service will not pay high wages. But what if you went to school and got a certificate to work specifically on Apple computers? Because there are less people qualified to work on Apple computers than those who can work on PC's, your ability will be specialized. It is a niche area that has a high demand and a low supply. This translates to higher pay.

The last thing to remember after you complete a full-proof marketing plan is that it may take a few tries. What's important is that you not give up! Freelancing is hard work with many challenges. Once things get flowing, things will get better. Don't let a set back or two get you down. Learn from your mistakes and use them to plunge forward. You will eventually succeed with the right plan. It may take some tinkering, but the payoff is well worth the hard work.

As you begin to do Freelancing you will want to focus on the jobs. This, of course, is your bread and butter. However, you must pay attention to your marketing strategy. Without a strong plan you will go through cycles of hot and cold. When you are hot and you have jobs, the money comes pouring in. But then, like a flash, you're back to that same old problem: no jobs, no money. You find yourself frantic and scrambling for that next job. You find one and accept whatever pay is offered just so you can make sure the lights stay on. Often times you undercut your usual price just to have work. Then you get a couple of jobs and the money is coming in again.

You don't need a weatherman to predict the hot and cold season for you. You need a good marketing plan to keep this from happening.

You have to set time aside to work on marketing yourself. It is essential for making your full-proof strategy work. When this is working you will always be hot because you will always be in demand. There will be no cold spells because you will have constant client inquiries asking for your services.

What is the secret of the full-proof marketing plan? First you find a way to get new clients. The next step will be to make those potential clients into sales. Finally you have to make those one time customers long term repeat customers.

Preparing Yourself for Freelancing

After you've carefully weighed all of your options and had a look at the market you'll see that it's quite extensive. Once you've decided on a few sites to sign up with a niche to specialize in you need to worry about putting yourself on the market for jobs and projects.

The first thing you need to worry about is your skills. Skills are the reason anyone hires you in the first place so these should be your main focus; they'll be the main focus of your potential clients.

Some people are born with obvious talent. They are born with gifts, which, because of their nature, make them known throughout the world. We have all heard of such greats as Einstein, Mozart, and Benjamin Franklin.

Most of us are not geniuses like these people. However, it is important to remember everyone is good at something. Some people are good with numbers. Others are more creative. Think about the things you can do. More importantly, think of things you like to do and are also good at. What are the areas where you excelled in school? Write down the skills you were born with.

Once you have figured out your natural skills you will have a starting place where you can begin creating your own career in freelancing. It is these skills that you want others to know about when you produce your resume. Besides the natural skills or talents you were born with think about those skills you have acquired throughout your life. Make a list of those skills. You may have learned these skills from higher education programs through colleges or trade schools. Have you earned a certification in any specific field? These are usually certificates of completion or achievement. Add any diplomas you have received. It does not matter so much where you got the diplomas. Of course it is impressive if you have a degree from Harvard but it is not necessary.

As you are developing your resume and beginning your career it might be an opportue time to think about getting more education in other areas. Again, it is the freedom to make your own hours as a freelancer that will give you the time you need to do such things as improve your education. Another advantage to modern technology is that of distance learning programs where you can work on line to earn a diploma or certification.

Take some time and think about how you can enhance your skills to make your career advance even farther. As a freelancer you are in control.

The next list you should make is all the experiences that have taught you skills throughout your life. Include jobs you have had in the past. Don't limit yourself to paid jobs. Add to this list any volunteer work you have done. Did you coordinate volunteers; did you put on a fundraiser; did you write articles about your event; what kind of planning did you do as a volunteer? Experience can enhance your sellability to clients. They want to know that you have the experience to complete the job they have requested.

Let's say you are asked to do a written piece on dogs. Your experience volunteering in an animal shelter for four years can give you the extra edge needed in order to win the job.

Go a step further in your list of experience. Each job gives you a wide range of experience within any given job. Write a job description of a particular job you have had and take a good look at all the skills you used when you did that job.

Clientele Acquisition Secrets

You have a plan of action but now you need some actual clients. The first step is determining what type of client actually needs your services. Depending on the type of service you offer, location may or may not have any bearing. If you're doing a programming or writing assignment that will be submitted via e-mail then distance is irrelevant. If you're offering to take senior prom pictures or paint murals then you'll have to carefully consider the location you market to. Sometimes being close to a potential client may be the thing that lands you a job. Keep that in mind when searching for a pool of potential clients.

A good place to start looking for local clients is a simple phone book. If you are looking for local business contacts that may use your area of expertise, finding them in the yellow pages may produce some leads. Alternatively there is an online version of the phone book at www.yellowpages.com. There may be directories of professional organizations where you can find potential customers. Other places to look are trade publications. Many of those publications contain lists of people that could be potential clients. You might also check and see what is happening in your particular area of interest. This can spark new ideas. It can also let you know what the latest trends are and the markets that are popular.

There are also companies that sell lists of names and addresses according to the criteria you give them. It can be expensive but may have a potentially high return.

What do you do now that you have your lists of potential clients? How do you reach them? One way is to call them. In certain freelance situations this can be a personal way to make contacts. You can also send them a letter in the mail. This is a relatively inexpensive way to generate clients and it can have good returns. You could also pay for advertising, but starting off this way can be costly. If your business grows larger and generates greater revenue, this may become a viable option.

There are different types of advertising. General advertising can reach a large audience but it is not necessarily always a target audience. If you want to reach a more specific audience you can run an advertisement in the classified sections of trade magazines. This is a more cost effective form of advertising rather than running big page advertisements. Often, if you run classified advertisements for a long period of time, you will get a discounted rate.

Sending mail directly to potential clients is specific and cost effective. You decide how your marketing dollars are directed which is straight at the companies that have the greatest potential for utilizing your skills. The larger the list of targets you have the greater the chance of success.

In order for direct mailing to work in marketing yourself you have to send out large numbers of direct mailings if you hope to get a response. On average, you might have a 1% to 2% response. That means you might get one customer out of about one hundred mailings. Direct mailings are not as effective as other forms of advertisements.

Once you have your target list, what should you send them? Well, you might only want to send a letter to those clients who are good possibilities but are not at the top of your list. Those at the top of list should get your resume, a business card and a cover letter. If you haven't bought business cards do so before you market yourself. You want a convenient way for your potential client to have your information readily accessible for any job that needs the skills you possess.

Your cover letter should be dynamic and attention getting. Don't send a boring pleading letter, hoping they will care. Send them a life line. Send them a letter that will make them sit up and take notice. Make yourself wanted as well as needed. The letter should clearly state the services you have to offer and why you are different from every other freelancer. Make sure that the person reading the cover letter knows why they should call you and hire you right away.

The next marketing strategy you can utilize is the telephone inquiry. These personal phone calls take finesse and planning. Not many people like sales calls. A strategy may be to send direct mailings to potential clients first and let them know you will be calling them. After a few days you can call the potential clients as a follow-up to the dynamic letter and resume you sent them. It acts as a prompt for a busy executive. Cold calling does not usually work as well as this type of strategy does.

There are more direct strategies that can be used to obtain new clients. One is networking. You can do this by doing some more research and finding out if there are any local organizations you can join in order to meet people to network with. The important thing is to make sure the group is a target group. You would not join a gardening group if you were doing computer graphics. While you may be lucky enough to find a potential client, it is not likely. A group of other computer artists or businesses that could use your services would be a much more valuable use of your time and marketing efforts.

Another situation to look for is any special events or seminars that target clients may be attending. For instance if you were that computer graphics freelancer you might want to set up a table at a computer seminar or sale.

Public relations campaigns are another way you can generate business. Again, do your research. Find an interesting way that magazines or newspapers might print an article featuring you that could generate business. This may be more difficult than the other marketing strategies suggested but if you can pitch it the right way the returns can be high and profitable.

Agencies do exist that you can pay to do your marketing. Beware. They can be very expensive. They usually take a percentage of your contract as their fee. It can be very sizable in some situations. You don't want to work for free. So be careful if you use them as your main strategy for generating new business.

Now let's now look at the possibilities for marketing online. The great part of online marketing is that it is often low cost and reaches a wide audience of potential customers worldwide.

ADVANCED TECHNIQUE: MAKING THE SALE

Now that you've completed your marketing campaign strategies you should be getting a few inquiries for your services. Have realistic expectations. Not every inquiry is going to be a sale. It does take work.

Marketing is only the first step. You have to make those marketing dollars and time pay off. You constantly need to seek ways of increasing your percentage of potential clients into real sales.

This increases your profit and ensures your freelancing business is a success. Your job is to convince those potential customers that you are the right person for the job and that their money will be well invested in you and your work.

First, make sure that the person you have been contacted by is a serious inquiry. Not all inquiries are. Some may only be curious browsers. In other situations the person you are communicating with is not the person who can actually approve the sale. They may not have the power to make decisions.

If a person makes an inquiry and is not offering an adequate compensation or you cannot fulfill the requirements of the project, then politely decline. You need to focus your energies on the serious inquiries. You need to make certain that you are talking to the right person. If possible, arrange a meeting with them. You want to talk to the person who can actually make a decision concerning a project. Your time is valuable, so there is no sense in spending unnecessary time with someone who cannot help you.

Once you have determined that you have an actual serious client and that they are the right person to speak to, then you must consider your first contact with them. The first contact can make or break a deal. In fact, in many circumstances a client decides within the first minute whether or not they will use you for a project.

More often than not your clients will want to contact you on the phone first. Keep these tips in mind when speaking with a client over the phone.

- Consider a second phone line or second cell phone that you only use for business purposes. This helps you separate business from personal work and the more organized you are the more successful you'll be.

- Answer the phone professionally and always be polite and attentive.

- The first time your customer or client contacts you, treat them like a customer. Once you've got to know your client well enough that they consider you a casual friend you can speak more casually but stick to formal talk at first.

- Answer the phone in a completely silent room. Background noise like children playing or the TV blaring gives you a sense of unprofessionalism and could negatively impact potential sales.

- Answer your calls with the name of your business, your name, and a request for how you can help the caller. "Good morning, this is the Freelance Production Company, this is Ed speaking, how may I help you." This lets the caller know you are a professional even though you may be the only person in the company.

- *Practice speaking.* Speak clearly and with confidence. Set a good, but not fast pace. There is nothing more annoying than talking to someone who is speaking so muffled or so rapidly that it is impossible to understand them. Remember, this is the first impression a potential client will have of you. Make it a positive experience. Remove any unnecessary language such as "umm." You can practice by recording some of your conversations and playing them back. Critique yourself and keep practicing! Have others listen to you and give you their feedback. There are books you can get that teach you breathing and diaphragm exercises that can greatly improve how you sound. The confidence in your voice will instill confidence in a potential client.

- Listen carefully to what your potential client is asking. Listening means clearing your mind from the slightest assumption that you know what your client wants and responding based on that assumption.

We live in an era where we are always in a hurry. The consensus seems to be the faster whatever it is can happen, the better. When you actually take the time to listen and respond to someone by repeating back to them what they are asking, chances are that that client will feel personally acknowledged.

They will know you understand what they need. Mr. Johnson, I understand that you are looking for someone to write a short book about your experience traveling through Ireland. You kept a diary and would like the personal experiences along with your traveling itinerary to be part of that writing. You would also like to add tips on how to save money. Is that correct so far, Mr. Johnson."

Below are suggestions for what to do when making contact through other mediums.

- Proceed with caution if your initial communication with a client is via e-mail. E-mail is extremely convenient and fast but since you're communicating though type you and your client have no subtle ways of conveying emotion so it's extremely easy for an e-mail to be misunderstood.

With the advent of the internet and, to a lesser extent, the advancement of cell phone technology, the art of writing has had a huge decline over the past few years. With email and chats online, a new kind of on- line short hand has emerged. It is a whole new way of corresponding, complete with its own unique language. While it may be tempting, you should avoid the use of modern short hand or "Chat speak." Never use acronyms or misspelled words in your letters. Imagine that you're going to show your letter to your High School English teacher. If you would receive anything less than an "A" then you need to rewrite it.

- **Research your potential client.**

The internet is a powerful and effective tool for doing research on your clients. Go to "advance search" in Google and type in their name. You will probably be amazed at the amount of information that comes up about them.

- **Arrange a face to face meeting**

If your potential client lives close enough. The internet will never replace what reading someone's body language can tell you about them. It makes it much easier to close a deal if you have this advantage. It also makes it easier to establish a long term relationship.

- **Bring or send samples of your work.** This should be part of your resume. If you are meeting your client face to face, bring the samples with you. If not, send your samples as quickly as possible. Remember to send samples that emphasize the type of work you want to do for the potential customer.

- **Arrive on time.** Remember the saying, "to be on time is to be early." Make sure you have plenty of time to arrive at your destination.

- **Get directions.** Map quest on line is a good way to do this.

- **Dress to impress.** Look like a professional at all times. Pick appropriate clothes to match your profession. Look clean and neat. A tidy haircut and a shave if you are a man, and natural looking makeup if you are a woman, will make a good first visual impression.

- Remember the first impression is the only one you will ever make so make sure it is your best.

- Thank your potential client for their time and consideration. Use language that indicates your willingness to help.

To add to the list of how to sell yourself to potential clients I have listed below the ten commandments of human relations. These are tried and true ways for freelancers, and for that matter, anyone looking for a job to make a good and lasting impression.

- **Speak to people.** There is nothing as nice as a cheerful word of greeting.

- **Smile at people.** It takes 72 muscles to frown, only 14 to smile.

- Make a conscious mental note to remember the name of the person you are speaking with and call them by their name as often as possible. The sweetest music to anyone's ears is the sound of her/his own name.

- **Be friendly and helpful.** If you want to have friends, be friendly yourself.

- **Be cordial.** Speak and act as if everything you do is a genuine pleasure.

- **Be genuinely interested in people.** You can like anybody if you try.

- **Be generous with praise** - cautious with criticism.

- Be considerate with the feelings of others. It will be appreciated.

- **Be thoughtful of the opinions of others.** There are three sides to a controversy: yours, the other person's, and the "right one".

- **Give excellent service.** What counts most in life is what we do for others.

Look at each one of these rules and try to review them every time you meet a new potential customer. It could mean money in the bank.

Don't pressure anyone into a sale. It may take more than one conversation for a customer to commit. Provide helpful suggestions and employ active listening. If they have an issue or problem, reflect it back to them to show you understand and are being attentive. At some point you will have to try and close the deal. If you have handled the rest of the suggestions appropriately, the closing of a sale should be easy and natural.

There may be, however, some objections made by the client. They need to be sure you will deliver what they want, when they want it, and that you are the person for the job. In these situations it is important to be more proactive then reactive. What this means is that you have thought ahead to what potential problems may arise and you have already worked out solutions before you even met with your potential customer. This means that you have to be empathetic. Empathetic means you have to try to be in your potential customer's position and think about what objections they might have.

Once you have worked your way through the objections and the deal looks like it is a success you move to the next component, taking the clients order. This means that you have the sale worked out and that the client is ready to buy. Sometimes this is a written order; sometimes it is a contract. Have the contract ready prior to the meeting. You can leave areas blank to write in the particulars. If there is a major revision to be done make sure you set a time to sign the contract in order to formally close the deal. If you do not have the order you may lose the sale. Be prepared. Be ready to close the deal before the negotiation begins.

If the client is still not completely ready to sign make them a trial offer to do some of the work as a sample for their approval. This enables the client to see what they are paying for with little risk. Once you produce the sample, you can set another meeting to get the order complete. Once a client is satisfied with your work, they are more likely to use you again. It is more profitable for both you and the client to develop a long term relationship rather than trying to find a new freelancer for every project they may have. That is why it is so vital to make a great first impression. It is not only to land the deal you are currently working on but to develop a regular influx of work.

Remember the old adage, "if at first you don't succeed, try, try again." Do not be discouraged if you are turned down for a job. See it as a learning opportunity. Try to review what you can do differently with the next potential customer. As you become more experienced and your reputation grows, so will your number of clients. Even though it can be discouraging don't give up. Nothing in life is "easy." It takes work but the rewards are numerous. So keep your head up and your goal in sight.

PAYMENT OPTIONS

Of all the things you'll consider while doing freelance work, possibly the most important one is how you'll get paid. There are a variety of methods but it depends mostly on whether or not you're using a freelancer website like Elance or vWorker and which particular website you use. We discussed this briefly in the previous section but it's worth some in-depth explanation and careful consideration.

Most freelancing websites have multiple options. These usually include: check by mail, money wire, direct deposit & PayPal. Of these methods I recommend direct deposit if and when it's available. Having the money directly deposited into your bank account is the safest and fastest way to get money from your freelance endeavors.

If your freelancing work is pulling in large amounts of money, over $100 per project or $200 per pay period, then you should stick to direct deposit, check by mail or money wire. As I said earlier, PayPal is convenient but has been known to have issues with holding money.

The payment method that usually generates the most questions is PayPal since it's the only purely-online method. Because of this the following chapter is dedicated mostly to information on how to use PayPal and the benefits of using PayPal.

The Ever-Popular PayPal

PayPal is an online payment system with a network of over 100 million users worldwide - currently the most popular funds transfer service on the Internet. PayPal allows businesses and individuals to transfer funds electronically between bank accounts and from credit or debit cards to bank accounts. Some of the common uses of PayPal's services include:

- Paying for online auctions (PayPal is owned by eBay)
- Purchase goods and services from online merchants

- Make donations or "good faith" payments
- Send cash to anyone with a PayPal account

A basic PayPal account is free. There are some fees associated with business accounts, but the good news for your customers is that they don't have to pay extra to make a purchase from you through PayPal. Anyone with a valid e-mail address can sign up for PayPal's services. From there, any number of checking accounts and credit or debit cards can be linked to the account. If there is more than one checking account or card associated with the account, users are given the option to choose which one will be used for each purchase or payment.

How it Works

For most businesses, a PayPal account acts as an intermediary between fund sources and bank accounts. When money is paid or transferred through PayPal, the funds reside in the PayPal account until you initiate a transfer to your checking account. Many online buyers, particularly those who frequent eBay, keep money in their PayPal accounts to make online spending easier.

If you decide to accept PayPal payments for your business, the first thing you'll need to do is open an account. You can start with a basic account, but you'll want to upgrade to either a Premier or a Business account as soon as possible. You can do this right from the start, or you can upgrade after your account is established.

To sign up, go to the PayPal home page and click on the "Sign up Now" button. You will be given the option to open a personal, business, or premier account (see the next section on what each account type offers). After you make your selection, you will be asked to enter some basic personal information: name, address, telephone number, and a valid e-mail address. The address you sign up with will be associated with the account, and customers can send you PayPal payments using this address.

Once the signup process is complete (and you have clicked on the link in your verification e-mail to return to the PayPal website), you will be asked if you would like to add a checking account or credit card to your account. You will likely want to add your checking account. Once it is verified, PayPal will display the verification on the payment page your customers see. This builds trust and confidence for your business.

When you enter your checking account information, PayPal will initiate two small deposits into your checking account (usually between 5 and 15 cents). The confirmation process involves checking your bank statements and entering these exact amounts at the PayPal website, which tells PayPal that you actually own the account. Once your checking account is verified, you can electronically transfer any PayPal funds received at no charge (the transfer process usually takes 3 to 4 business days).

If you don't want to transfer funds into your checking account, or you want occasional faster access to your PayPal account, you can apply for a free PayPal debit card or business Visa, which can be used anywhere credit cards are accepted. The PayPal card draws from your account; the credit card is a regular Visa with a PayPal logo added.

What is the difference between the types of PayPal accounts available? Here is what each one involves:

Available PayPal Accounts Personal

- Free to open, no monthly fees
- Send and receive money

- Shop online with eBay and merchants who accept PayPal
- Accept a limited number of credit card payments per year.

Premier
- All features of Personal account
- eBay tools and merchant services
- Accept credit, debit, and bank account payments

Business
- All features of Premier account
- PayPal ATM/debit card included
- Multi-user access

Transaction Fees

PayPal recently change the way it charges transaction fees and now all accounts have the exact same transaction fees (which pretty much solidifies that, as a freelancer, you only need a Premier account). All credit card transfers are charged 30 cents plus 2.9%. This means if you sell something for $100 and they buy via PayPal then your net profit will be $96.80 ($100 minus 2.9% is 97.10, minus 30 cents and you get $96.80)

Unlike merchant accounts, PayPal does not require a long-term contract, setup fees, or monthly, startup, or cancellation fees.

Standard Website Payments and Off Line Options

As with other PayPal methods, there are no additional fees associated with this package. Website Payments Standard can be integrated with an existing shopping cart, and allows your customers to pay through PayPal even if they don't have a PayPal account themselves.

For $20 per month, you can add the option to accept credit cards by phone, fax, mail, or in person with PayPal's Virtual Terminal service. This feature is included in the PayPal Website Payments Pro package.

PayPal Website Payments Pro

This package includes all the features of the Standard package, and also provides the features of merchant accounts and gateways for less money. The Pro package is currently the only PayPal plan with a monthly fee ($20), but again requires no contract, startup or termination fees. The Virtual Terminal is included with this system, and it is recommended that you use a shopping cart system already integrated with Website Payments Pro. You can find a directory of PayPal-ready shopping carts here: http://solutions.paypal.com/procarts/

PayPal E-mail Payments

This is a professional invoicing system available free with a Premier or Business account. You can send e-mail invoices to your customers, who then pay by clicking on the link within the message.

The invoicing system is easy to set up (it takes about ten minutes) and customers do not need a PayPal account to make payments. You can also add Virtual Terminal to this service for $20 a month.

Other PayPal Payment Options

If you already accept credit cards on your website, or you decide to sign up for a merchant account or other third-party processing service, you can add PayPal as an additional option for your customers. Typically, this is accomplished with customizable buttons you can install on your website (PayPal will generate the HTML code for you). When a customer clicks on the button, they will be taken to a page hosted on the PayPal server to sign in to their PayPal account.

Many Internet consumers who already use PayPal for eBay and other purchases may prefer this option, and you can increase your sales by adding a PayPal option to your website.

How PayPal Profits

PayPal might seem like a delightfully pleasant company that offers all sorts of free services but, like any major company, they must make money as well. PayPal's profit system is arranged similarly to that of a bank: they earn interest from the "float" of the funds they manage. With over 100 million accounts, there are always funds sitting in some of them earning interest for PayPal.

Of course, they also profit from the transaction fees and the monthly fees for their Virtual Terminal service. PayPal is unique in that it was the first funds transfer company created specifically to service the Internet. Their commitment to quality and service has allowed them to become one of the giants of e-commerce.

Things to Watch out For

As I mentioned before, PayPal has a bit of a reputation when it comes to certain types of Internet business. If PayPal thinks that you've broken their terms in any way they may immediately close your PayPal account. That, however, is far from the worst part.

When PayPal closes your account they also put a hold on all of your funds. Every payment that has been made to you is immediately frozen and kept under the authority of PayPal. They do this for as long as 180 days or 6 months.

If you're just supplementing your daily income with freelance work this may not be an issue. If you're making a living from freelancing then having your funds held for 6 month may be as good as a death sentence.

What seems to particularly spark PayPal's nasty side is any website promotion or advertisement that has to do with Internet Marketing or promotes that buyers and clients can make money or attain a specific level of success.

As a freelance worker this is not an issue you will likely have to deal with. Most of the time, you'll be using Freelance websites who go through PayPal; so you should be immune to this problem. If you offer your freelance work through your own website, however, you should really avoid PayPal if at all possible because the potential risks may outweigh the benefits. Also if you have an extremely profitable business making 20,000 or more per month you are given a dedicated PayPal representative. Do not assume that his or her approval of your website will ever guarantee anything; reps do not have the final word.

What's Next?

If you've read this far then you've got the tools you need to succeed as a freelancer.

Tips and Final Thoughts

The following pieces of advice will be invaluable for furthering and maintaining your freelancing career. Study this section carefully.

Be a Professional

Companies and individuals don't have a hard time spotting fakes and fools. You're not going to earn their respect or their repeat business unless you act like a professional. That means sounding professional and looking professional. Sometimes business requires investment; just because you *can* do everything yourself doesn't mean you *should* do everything yourself. The one thing I find people skimping out on is their presentation. Your website, your demos, your portfolio, really everything about you must look professional. If there's some aspect of your marketing that you can't do extremely well yourself then hire yourself a freelancer to do it.

Aside from sounding and looking professional you need to act professional. This doesn't mean you should become an emotionless automaton. Be personal and approachable. If you show that you care and enjoy what you do, your clients will be able to see that as well. Keep your skills honed. Take opportunities to sharpen them. Keep up on current trends and information in the field you choose to work in. Your clients will be impressed on how up-to-date you are and how much expert knowledge you have.

Do Your Homework

One of the best ways to become a successful business is to research successful companies in your chosen field. Ask other professionals what they have done to become successful. You save a lot of time if you don't have to reinvent the wheel. Learn from other people's successes and failures. The information can be invaluable.

Another way to evaluate your services is to send out brief surveys when you complete a job. The feedback can open avenues to areas where you need improvement. Negative feedback is always an opportunity to make change. You can take the positive comments and use them in your advertising.

You can even evaluate your clients. Prioritize them. Which ones are the best clients and which ones take up all your time? Consider increasing your rates to see if those using all of your time meet the challenge. They will either pay you more and make it worth your while or they won't come back. That way you can concentrate on your money makers. Remember, if a customer is wasting your time then they are wasting your money.

Nobody Likes a Work-Addict

Don't overwork yourself. It may seem noble to try to do as many jobs as possible but not if you risk burn out. To make matters worse the quality of your work may suffer and your clients may notice. In the long term you could lose work by trying to do too much.

As a freelancer you have the power to decide how hard you work but you'll also be presented with more opportunities to overwork yourself than ever. You need to take care of yourself. If you are trying to do too much, you are not taking care of yourself. Besides, what fun would it be to be working all of the time? Didn't you want to become a freelancer so you could make your own schedule and spend more time with family and friends?

If you have made some contacts networking you may want to make deals about sending each other work when you are overloaded. If mutually agreed upon, it can keep the jobs flowing but will create a stop gap when there is too much.

If it is cost effective, you may want to hire someone who can take on some of your duties such as web site maintenance, answering phones, and taking care of the financial aspects so that you can concentrate on other projects. This can save you time and prevent burnout.

One Very Important Word: NO!

Go ahead and practice saying it. Say it to yourself in the mirror.

Get used to being able to say it without hesitation or over analysis. Just because a client offers you a job does not mean you have to take it. Is the job something you can do? Does the job fit into your overall plan of acquiring a long term client? Think of the job as a step in the road to the million dollars you seek. Also consider what would happen if you did not take the job. It is not always prudent to take on a job just because it meets the short term goal of a paycheck. If it does not pay well or the client is not likely to be a repeat customer, then politely decline. Again, you have to manage your time and resources wisely. You need to pick your clients and jobs wisely as well.

Invest Wisely in Your Marketing Strategy

A way to utilize your marketing time and dollars is to think of unusual ways to attract the attention of potential new clients. You need to set yourself apart. What do your mailings look like? Are you using eye-catching colors, words, and images that will attract a potential client's attention? You don't want your mailings to automatically be thrown in the trash. If you can get a potential client to spend a minute paying attention to your marketing attempt, you are halfway to winning them over.

Another way to make the most of your marketing dollars is to collaborate with other companies. Working together can be an effective way for both of you to get your names out there and known. When you split the price you both win. You are able to send materials out to more people and have greater results working together than you might have just trying to do it on your own.

Try to utilize your marketing ideas for certain occasions or events. If you can coordinate your marketing with ongoing events you may reach a wider range of prospects.

Look at your website and explore its potential. Look at how you can raise your ranks in search engines as mentioned in a previous chapter. If you can increase your ranking you can definitely get more hits on your site when people are searching for the kind of services you offer.

Think About Your Clients

Have you considered how long it might take for a person to be able to load your webpage? Not everyone has lightning fast internet service. If you have a lot of graphics and they have a lot of megabytes, you may want to consider choosing other graphics or eliminating them all together. The longer it takes a potential customer to load your site, the more likely they are to skip it for the next site on their search engine results. Don't have a whole lot of glitz and fanfare. Make your website easy to access and easy to navigate. Make sure it gets to the point and that your contact information is current and easy to access. It may even be one of the questions you add to your survey. You can ask a client whether or not the website was useful and what you could do to improve it.

Make a habit of updating your site. Give your clients something to look at that is different so that they will come back. Post promotions, deals and some new examples of your work. Don't let your site sit and get old and filled with cobwebs. It is your store front and sweeping and the occasional touch up paint should be part of your regular routine.

Get to know your customers. If you know a client's birthday, send them a card or email. You can even offer a discount as a birthday gift.

Always listen to your customers. Be polite and empathetic. Get to know their likes, dislikes and idiosyncrasies. Write them down in a file to help you remember. Paying attention to a client's needs gives you a much better chance of keeping them as a long term customer. Always make sure your customers have access to you. Give them your phone numbers and let them know the best time to reach you. The trust it builds with customers can mean dollars to you. Customers who trust you will continue give you jobs.

My last little piece of advice is to always thank your customers.

The most common way is to send a cordial thank-you email or even snail-mail them a thank-you card. The purpose of this is that it encourages them to be a repeat customer. If they feel they have been taken care of than they are more likely to take of you in the future. Ever heard the phrase, "You scratch my back, I'll scratch yours"?

LAST BUT NOT LEAST

So, what do you think? Are you ready to get out there and start making money as a freelancer? If you've been paying attention to this book you should have acquired all the skills you need and have all the reference necessary to develop a healthy freelancing career. You might never want to back to "the grind" again.

Eventually you might be able to start your own business and hire your own employees. Once your freelancing takes off and you start getting more offers than you can possibly hand, it's the next logical step. Many of today's famous and extremely wealthy entrepreneurs and business people started out their careers doing freelance work and slowly built up an empire. The beautiful thing about freelance work is that the possibilities are truly limitless; only your talents, skills and work ethics determine the ultimate quality of your experience. So don't let the economy get you down; don't stress over a crummy job or feel despair because you don't have any job - make your own job! Become a freelancer and discover the power, freedom and success that you never thought possible!

www.ingramcontent.com/pod-product-compliance
Ingram Content Group UK Ltd.
Pitfield, Milton Keynes, MK11 3LW, UK
UKHW022212230426
12048UKWH00016BA/801